To Kurt, Rebecca

may you grow up

in peace,

Barbara Sofer

Jerusalem 1999

Shalom, Haver

שלום חבר

Goodbye, Friend

by Barbara Sofer

Hebrew translation by Shulamith Basok
Designed by Madeline Wikler

KAR-BEN COPIES • ROCKVILLE, MD

With gratitude to Rachel Rabin
for sharing your photos and memories.
— B.S.

Library of Congress Cataloging-in-Publication Data

Sofer, Barbara
    Shalom, haver = Goodbye, friend / by Barbara Sofer.
        p. cm.
    Summary: A photo essay in memory of Yitzhak Rabin, the Israeli
prime minister who was assassinated in l995.
    ISBN 0-929371-97-6
    1. Rabin, Yitzhak, 1922-1995 —Pictorial works — Juvenile literature.
2. Prime ministers — Israel — Pictorial works — Juvenile literature.
[1. Rabin, Yitzhak, 1922-1995. 2. Prime ministers. 3. Jews-Biography.]
I. Title.
DS126.6.R32S64 1996
956.9405'092—dc20
[B]   96-7065
                                        CIP
                                        AC

Published by KAR-BEN COPIES, INC. Rockville, MD 1-800-4KARBEN
Printed in the United States of America.

YITZHAK RABIN ■ 1922-1995

How do you say goodbye to a friend?

אֵיךְ אוֹמְרִים שָׁלוֹם לְחָבֵר?

You remember.

אַתָּה זוֹכֵר.

You remember him
as a kid just like you,

אַתָּה זוֹכֵר אוֹתוֹ כְּיֶלֶד כָּמוֹךָ,

With a mom,

עִם אִמָּא,

a dad,

אַבָּא,

and a little sister Rachel
who liked to tag along.

וְאָחוֹת קְטַנָּה הַדְּבֵקָה בּוֹ.

In school and camp
בְּבֵית-סֵפֶר וּבְקַיְטָנָה,

he played soccer,
learned scouting,

הוּא שִׂחֵק כַּדּוּרֶגֶל,
לָמַד פְּעוּלוֹת צוֹפִיּוֹת,

and took long hikes with his friends.

וְיָצָא לְטִיּוּלִים אֲרֻכִּים בְּמֶרְחֲבֵי הַטֶּבַע.

You remember how brave he was.

אַתָּה זוֹכֵר כַּמָּה אַמִּיץ הוּא הָיָה.

He studied to be a farmer,
but Israel needed him to be a soldier.

הוּא לָמַד לִהְיוֹת חַקְלַאי,
אֲבָל לִמְדִינַת יִשְׂרָאֵל הָיָה דָרוּשׁ חַיָל.

He married Leah, who was also a soldier.

הוּא נָשָׂא לְאִשָּׁה אֶת הַחַיֶּלֶת לֵאָה.

They had two children, Yuval and Dalia.

נוֹלְדוּ לָהֶם יְלָדִים, יוּבַל וְדַלְיָה.

He became commander
of Israel's army.

הוּא מֻנָּה לְרַמַטְכָּ"ל,
מְפַקֵּד כָּל הַצָּבָא.

and led his country to victory.

וְהוֹבִיל אֶת מְדִינָתוֹ לְנִצָּחוֹן.

As ambassador for Israel he met world leaders,
but wherever he went he liked to talk to children.

כְּשֶׁהָיָה שַׁגְרִיר שֶׁל מְדִינַת יִשְׂרָאֵל הוּא פָּגַשׁ מַנְהִיגִים מִכָּל
הָעוֹלָם. בְּכָל מָקוֹם הוּא אָהַב לְשׂוֹחֵחַ עִם יְלָדִים.

At home he had fun with his grandchildren,
and sometimes found time for tennis.

בַּבַּיִת הִשְׁתַּעֲשַׁע וּמָצָא גַם פְּנַאי לְשַׂחֵק טֶנִיס.

How do you say goodbye to a friend?

אֵיךְ אוֹמְרִים שָׁלוֹם לְחָבֵר?

You think about all he achieved.

אַתָּה חוֹשֵׁב עַל כָּל הֶשֵּׂגָיו.

As Prime Minister he welcomed new immigrants,

כְּשֶׁהוּא נִבְחַר לִהְיוֹת רֹאשׁ מֶמְשָׁלָה הוּא בֵּרַךְ עוֹלִים חֲדָשִׁים,

and went all the way to China to make friends for Israel.

וְהִרְחִיק לֶכֶת עַד סִין כְּדֵי לִמְצוֹא לְיִשְׂרָאֵל חֲבֵרִים חֲדָשִׁים.

He shook hands with enemies
because he believed in peace.

הוּא לָחַץ יָדַיִם לְאוֹיְבִים

מִפְּנֵי שֶׁהוּא הֶאֱמִין בַּחֲשִׁיבוּת הַשָּׁלוֹם.

He signed agreements
with Israel's neighbors,

הוּא חָתַם עַל חוֹזֵי-שָׁלוֹם
עִם שְׁכֵנֶיהָ שֶׁל יִשְׂרָאֵל,

and received the Nobel Peace Prize.

וְקִבֵּל אֶת פְּרַס נוֹבֵל לְשָׁלוֹם.

How do you say goodbye to a friend?

אֵיךְ אוֹמְרִים שָׁלוֹם לְחָבֵר?

You remember things
that made you laugh.

אַתָּה זוֹכֵר דְּבָרִים מַצְחִיקִים.

Once he forgot his bowtie
and had to borrow one
from President Clinton.

פַּעַם אַחַת הוּא הָיָה צָרִיךְ
לְבַקֵּשׁ מֵהַנָּשִׂיא קְלִינְטוֹן עֲנִיבָה,
כִּי הוּא שָׁכַח לְהָבִיא אֶת שֶׁלּוֹ.

You remember things that made you angry.
You were angry when you heard he was killed.

אַתָּה זוֹכֵר דְּבָרִים שֶׁהִכְעִיסוּ אוֹתְךָ.
הָיִיתָ אָבֵל כְּשֶׁהוּא נֶהֱרַג.

And you were sad as you watched so many people
walk past his coffin to say goodbye.

הָיִיתָ עָצוּב כְּשֶׁצָפִיתָ בָּאֲנָשִׁים הָרַבִּים
שֶׁעָבְרוּ עַל פְּנֵי אֲרוֹנוֹ.

They lit candles.

הִדְלִיקוּ נֵרוֹת.

Drew pictures.

צִיְרוּ תְּמוּנוֹת.

Prayed.

הִתְפַּלְלוּ.

And sang in soft, sad voices.　　וְשָׁרוּ בְּקוֹל שָׁקֵט וְעָצוּב.

Leaders from many lands
came to Jerusalem to say goodbye.

מַנְהִיגִים מֵהַרְבֵּה אֲרָצוֹת
בָּאוּ לִירוּשָׁלַיִם לוֹמַר שָׁלוֹם לֶחָבֵר.

His family was saddest of all.

מִשְׁפַּחְתּוֹ הָיְתָה עֲצוּבָה מִכֻּלָּם.

How do you say goodbye to a friend?

אֵיךְ אוֹמְרִים שָׁלוֹם לְחָבֵר?

You promise to remember.
You promise to work for peace.
Because in Hebrew shalom means
both goodbye and peace.

אַתָּה מַבְטִיחַ לְעַצְמְךָ לִזְכֹּר,
מַבְטִיחַ לִפְעוֹל לְמַעַן שָׁלוֹם.
וְאַתָּה זוֹכֵר שֶׁהַמִּלָּה שָׁלוֹם הִיא בְּרָכָה
וְגַם מִלַּת פְּרֵידָה.

Shalom, haver.

שָׁלוֹם חָבֵר.

MY BROTHER YITZHAK

Many of the early photographs in this book came from Yitzhak Rabin's sister Rachel. As we turned the pages of her albums, she shared memories of her brother.

"Yitzhak was born in Jerusalem, but we grew up in Tel Aviv. Our home was simple—we didn't even own a radio.

"In school lunch was a class project. We grew the vegetables, cooked, and cleaned up. Both of our parents were involved in the community, so Yitzhak had to babysit for me after school. Most days we played outside until dark—hide and seek and ball games. Sometimes, when his friends had a party, he'd ask the girls in the neighborhood to keep an eye on me. They're still my friends today.

"Yitzhak was quiet and shy, and he liked to invite his friends over rather than go to visit them. I was talkative and always wanted to tag along.

"When we were kids, I never expected he'd be a leader. In elementary school, there are two types of leaders: the troublemaker and the talker. Yitzhak was neither. He was thoughtful and good-hearted, and someone the other kids respected. He joined the army as a private but quickly rose to commander. I was in a secret course for wireless operators, and he was in another army course, and we passed notes back and forth. Both of us married the same week —when there was a lull in the fighting.

"I went to live on Kibbutz Manara in the North. Yitzhak would visit me whenever he could. I was proud when he became Chief of Staff and later Prime Minister. I went to Oslo when he won the the Nobel Peace Prize. When I turned 70, I took our grandchildren on a tour of our old neighborhood, and Leah made us a family dinner.

"I worried about my brother. But he couldn't believe that after all he'd been through, he would be killed by one of our own people. It's still hard for me to believe that such a horrendous thing could happen.

"I've been a teacher much of my life and I'm glad that this book will help children learn about my brother."